CATS
SET II

Balinese Cats

Stuart A. Kallen
ABDO & Daughters

visit us at
www.abdopub.com

Published by Abdo & Daughters, 4940 Viking Drive, Suite 622, Edina, Minnesota 55435.
Copyright © 1998 by Abdo Consulting Group, Inc., Pentagon Tower, P.O. Box 36036,
Minneapolis, Minnesota 55435 USA. International copyrights reserved in all countries.
No part of this book may be reproduced in any form without written permission from the
publisher.

Printed in the United States.

Photo credits: Peter Arnold, Inc., Animals Animals

Edited by Lori Kinstad Pupeza

Library of Congress Cataloging-in-Publication Data

Kallen, Stuart., 1955-
    Balinese cats / Stuart A. Kallen.
    p.   cm. -- (Cats. Set II)
    Includes index.
    Summary: Describes the physical characteristics, behavior, and life cycle of
    these long-haired graceful cats.
    ISBN 1-56239-579-3
    1. Balinese cat--Juvenile literature. [1. Balinese cats. 2. Cats.] I. Title. II.
    Series: Kallen, Stuart A., 1955- Cats. Set II.
    SF449.B34K35   1998
    636.8'3--dc20   95-48191
                                                             CIP
                                                             AC

Contents

Lions, Tigers, and Cats

Few animals are as beautiful and graceful as cats. And all cats are related. From the wild lions of Africa to common house cats, all belong to the family *Felidae*. Wild cats are found almost everywhere. They include cheetahs, jaguars, lynx, ocelots, and **domestic** cats.

Cats were first domesticated around 5,000 years ago in the Middle East. Although tamed by humans, house cats still think and act like their bigger cousins.

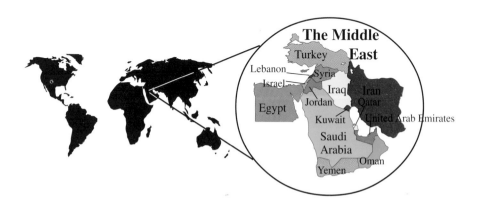

All cats are related to each other.

Balinese Cats

Balinese cats are like Siamese cats with long hair. The first longhaired Siamese were discovered in the 1950s. As more and more longhaired Siamese were born, they began to attract a following among cat lovers. These beautiful cats were given the name Balinese.

The cats are as graceful and **agile** as dancers. The name comes from the dancers on the island of Bali in Indonesia. Balinese cats with tortoiseshell, lynx, or red markings are called Javanese. The **Cat Fanciers Association** accepted Balinese for championship status in 1970.

Balinese have the same features as Siamese except for their longer, more silky hair.

*Balinese cats are a lot
like Siamese cats.*

Qualities

Balinese are eager, lively, and affectionate. It's hard to keep a secret from a Balinese. A Balinese will stick its nose into any activity that's going on around it. While not as noisy as their Siamese cousins, Balinese still love to "talk." They also love to play and jump. Balinese are sleek, **lithe**, and graceful.

Like all cats, Balinese cats are curious and will pounce on anything that moves. Their quick movements and sharp eyesight allow them to be adventuresome and have good hunting skills.

Opposite page: Balinese are known for being unusually curious.

Coat and Color

There are four basic types of Balinese cats. Seal points have cream coats with seal-brown markings. Blue points have bluish-white coats with deep-blue markings. Chocolate points have ivory coats with chocolate-brown markings. Lilac points have off-white coats with frosty-gray markings.

Javanese patterns include red, tortoiseshell, and lynx point. All Balinese cats have almond-shaped, bright blue eyes. Their fur may grow up to two inches (five cm) in length.

Opposite page: A Balinese cat.

Size

The Balinese is medium in size, weighing between 5 and 10 pounds (2 to 4.5 kg). Its body is long, slender, and well muscled. The head is a long, tapering wedge with large, wide ears. Their legs are long and thin and their paws are dainty, small, and oval.

Balinese cats have smooth, graceful movements. Their slender bodies are big enough to kill small animals, but little enough to hide from their **prey**. Their tiny paws make very little noise so their prey can't hear them coming.

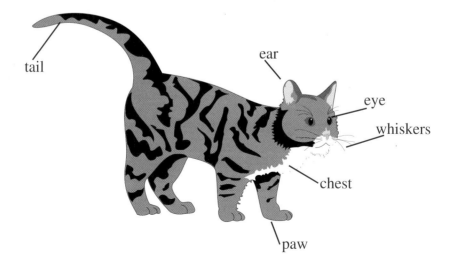

tail

ear

eye

whiskers

chest

paw

Balinese will grow to between 5 and 10 pounds (2 to 4.5 kg).

Care

Like any pet, a Balinese cat needs a lot of love and attention. Balinese cats make fine pets. But they still have some of their wild instincts. Cats are natural hunters and do well exploring outdoors.

A **scratching post** where the cat can sharpen its claws saves furniture from damage. A cat buries its waste and should be trained to use a litter box. The box needs to be cleaned every day. Cats lick their coats to stay clean. Balinese cats have long hair that will need a regular brushing. This will keep the cat from swallowing hair balls and becoming ill. Balinese cats love to play. A ball, **catnip**, or a loose string will keep a kitten busy for hours.

Cats should be **spayed** or **neutered** unless you are planning to breed them. Females can have dozens of kittens in a year. Males will spray very unpleasant odors indoors and out if not fixed.

Balinese cats love to play.

Feeding

Cats are meat eaters. Hard bones that do not splinter help keep a cat's teeth and mouth clean. If a cat lives outside, it will hunt for birds or rodents. It will provide for itself with a good diet.

Most cats live indoors. Water should always be available. Most cats survive fine on dried cat food. They like **catnip** and other treats. Although they love milk, it often causes cats to become ill.

Dry cat food is just fine for most cats.

Kittens

A female cat is **pregnant** for about 65 days. When kittens are born, there may be from two to eight babies. The average cat has four to six kittens.

Kittens are blind and helpless for the first several weeks. They are born creamy white and will get more color after a few weeks. After about three weeks kittens will start crawling and playing. At this time they may be given cat food. After about a month, kittens will run, wrestle, and play games.

If the cat is a **pedigree**, it should be **registered** and given papers at this time. At 10 weeks the kittens are old enough to be sold or given away.

Opposite page: The average cat has four to six kittens.

Buying a Kitten

The best place to get a Balinese cat is from a breeder. Cat shows are also good places to find kittens. Next you must decide if you want a simple pet or a show winner. A basic Balinese can cost $50. A blue-ribbon winner could cost as much as $1,000. When you buy a Balinese, you should get **pedigree** papers that **register** the animal with the **Cat Fanciers Association**.

When buying a kitten, check it closely for signs of good health. The ears, nose, mouth, and fur should be clean. Its eyes should be bright and clear. The cat should be alert and interested in its surroundings. A healthy kitten will move around with its head held high.

Healthy Balinese kittens will be playful and fun.

Glossary

agile - able to move quickly and easily.

breed/official breed - a kind of cat, a Balinese is a breed of cat. An official breed is a breed that is recognized by special cat organizations.

Cat Fanciers Association - a group that sets the standards for the breeds of cats.

catnip - the dried leaves and stems of a plant of the mint family, used as a stuffing for cats' toys because cats are stimulated by and drawn to its strong smell.

domestic/domesticated - tamed or adapted to home life.

Felidae - Latin name given to the cat family.

lithe - bending easily, flexible.

neutered - a male cat that is neutered cannot get a female cat pregnant.

pedigree - an official list of a cat's ancestors.

pregnant - when a female cat has kittens inside her.

prey - an animal that is hunted for food. A bird might be a cat's prey.

register - to add a cat to a list of names of its breed.

scratching post - a post for a cat to scratch on, which is usually made out of wood or covered with carpet, so the cat can wear down its nails.

spayed - a female cat that is spayed cannot have kittens.

Internet Sites

All About Cats
http://w3.one.net/~mich/index.html
See pictures of cats around the net, take a cat quiz to win prizes, and there is even a cat advice column. This is a fun and lively site.

Cat Fanciers Website
http://www.fanciers.com/
Information on breeds, shows, genetics, breed rescue, catteries and other topics. This is a very informative site, including clubs and many links.

Cats Homepage
http://www.cisea.it/pages/gatto/meow.htm
Page for all cat lovers. Cat photo gallery, books and more. This site has music and chat rooms, it's a lot of fun.

Cats Cats Cats
http://www.geocities.com/Heartland/Hills/5157/
This is just a fun site with pictures of cats, links, stories, and other cat stuff.

These sites are subject to change. Go to your favorite search engine and type in CATS for more sites.

PASS IT ON

Tell Others Something Special About Your Pet

To educate readers around the country, pass on interesting tips about animals, maybe a fun story about your animal or pet, and little unknown facts about animals. We want to hear from you!

To get posted on ABDO & Daughters website, E-mail us at "animals@abdopub.com"

Index